MW00938886

MAN
RULES

Manly Advice - For a Manly Life

Earl Pitts

with Gary Burbank and Tim Mizak

ISBN: 1503249891
ISBN-13: 978-1503249899

ACKNOWLEDGMENTS

This book is dedicated to our families - for not rolling their eyes - even after hearing these for thirty years.

To - JD, Rocco, Rob, Jim, Kel and William - for their continued work at The Duck Inn.

And especially to all the idiots, chuckle-heads, useless pant-loads, lying weasels, twisted nimrods, halfwits, bone-heads, jerks and knuckle-dragging mouth-breathers in the world who continue to do what they do - and make us crazy enough to complain about it.

If you get first pick -
always take Superman.

The sun sets every day of your life -
so don't go all soft and squishy
when you see one.

If you're angry - always count to ten
before acting.
Unless you're going to smack someone.
then do it on 'three'.

The three magic words are -
'I Love You'.
Or,
"Kiss My Ass!'
Depending on the situation.

MAN RULE # 113

Never ask a man to get excited about a baby.

You know what makes me sick? You know what makes me so mad I just wanna put a bunch a bug-zappers in Disneyworld - and hopefully finally get rid of that dang Tinkerbell??

I think we have talked at length about the differences between your male and your female of the species. Everybody agrees... your man and your woman are different. You don't have to go to Venus or Mars to figure that out.

Here's where I went to find out - church. Yeah - we were down at the church Sunday, and this young couple in our congregation brought in a new baby they just hatched. Lord - you would have thought Elvis had come back to life and walked down the center aisle. I mean - it looked like Walmart on Thanksgiving night. There was a mad woman-rush to see this new baby.

Now - when a man sees a brand new baby....he's more liable to actually back up a little. A man will tend to look at a new baby like he looks at a deadly animal in the zoo- from a safe distance.

Best I can tell - it's a hormone thing. When a woman sees a new baby - she gets all stupid.

First of all... she's gonna tell the new mama it is the cutest baby she has ever seen in her entire life. Which is mathematically impossible.

And then - all of a sudden, this grown up woman you spent half your life with - will start speaking in tongues. She will start babbling in baby talk. 'Look at the cutesy-wutesy toesy-woesies...' 'Look at the little finger-wingers.' And you're left to wonder - 'What happened to my old lady's brainsy-wainsy?'

Then she takes a sniff and goes, 'Who made a 'stinky-winky'? And I go - 'Oops, sorry, Pearl - that was me.' Yeah - she doesn't think it's funny when I rip one.

And when it comes to holding the baby. Women will get into a flat-out cage-match fight to hold a baby first. Ask a man to hold a new baby - and he'll hold it like the bomb squad holds a suspicious package. Which would be appropriate - because this thing could go off at any second.

Wake up, America! Man Rule #113 - No - I do not want to hold the baby. I said, *NO* - I do not want to hold the baby!! I swear - if you give me the baby - I am going to throw it. Thank you. I'm Earl Pitts, American. Pitts Off!

**'Maybe it's just me... but every new-born baby looks
a little bit like Yoda.
I mean, if he wasn't green.'**

MAN RULE # 82

Eating in the car

You know what makes me sick? You know what makes me so mad I just wanna go to a cannibal convention - with giant onion rings around my neck?

Sometimes I get a little misty-eyed when I think about the good old days. I mean - there were things we used to do back in the day - we don't do no more. And that's sad. The world's getting faster...and we're losing some of our humanity.

Like - I thought about this driving through the McDonald's last night. You know what you don't see no more? You don't see a family sitting in their car eating no more.

No sir - you eat while you're driving. Or... you take it home and eat it. There used to be a time when a family saw the value of sitting in a parking lot and eating in a car. That was your family values right there.

I mean - that's your quality family time. Kids in the back seat - throwing French fries at each other. Mom's got a milkshake up on the dashboard. Dad's got his nugget dipping sauce balanced between his knees. Yeah - you don't see families today taking the time to eat together and bond together like that anymore. And that is a shame.

I remember my Daddy used to take us out on Friday night to the Red Barn. And we'd set there in the car, eating Barnbusters. We'd be thinking that was how the Rockefellers must have lived. And then the whole rest of the weekend - that car used to smell like onion rings and secret sauce.

You know... they got fast food... and they got casual food. And now they come up with something called fast casual. What I miss - is fast redneck casual food in the back seat of a car.

Wake up, America. Man Rule #82 - Bring back American values . Throw your kids in the car tonight... and eat in the Wendy's parking lot. And tell'em Earl sent you. I'm Earl Pitts American. Pitts Off!

'Eating while driving is fine. Except for maybe a plate of spaghetti.'

MAN RULE # 214

No real man owns a closet he can walk in to.

You know what makes me sick? You know what makes me so mad I just wanna go skinny-dipping in a leech-filled swamp?

I was coming up with a list the other night of all the reasons I hate rich people. They got nice cars and a helluva lot nicer houses than we do. They got power. They go on fancy vacations. They eat in restaurants where they put more silverware in front of you - than the rest of us even own!!

And don't get me wrong. I do not begrudge your rich people being rich. No - I believe in the American dream. I believe anybody with two bucks in their pocket - a dream - and a liberal application of sweat - can make it in this country.

But here's the thing that grips me by the short-hairs about rich people. Walk-in closets.

Okay - I have seen rich people's closets on the TV and in movies. They are not closets. They are rooms - for clothes. Yeah - rich people's pants... got their own room!! I seen this one guy's closet on the TV... he had more light-bulbs in his closet - than we do in our whole dang house!!

You know what we got? A hole in the wall - with sliding mirrors in front of it. One door fell off ten years ago and is still in the garage.   The other's still up - but it don't slide no more. So you kind of got to get dressed around it. Yeah - and we got so much clothes jammed in there... some day - one of us gonna yank on the wrong hanger - and I pity the people in the immediate blast zone.

And there's you rich people -rubbing your walk-in closets with their ample and convenient space in our faces. A poor woman will look at pictures of a walk-in closet... and she'll get glassy-eyed and her mind will go off to some fantasy place.   Kind of like a man will look at pictures of Kate Upton.   Might as well dream - too... cause it won't never happen in real life.

Wake up, America! Man Rule #214 -   No real man needs a giant walk-in closet. But we would like one big enough to hide in when we hear the killer breaking in the house. Me and my old lady are way passed squeezing under the bed. I'm Earl Pitts, American. Pitts Off!

'My old lady told me to look in the closet and take everything I don't wear to Goodwill.
So I took all of her clothes. Yeah, it struck me as a funny request.'

MAN RULE # 17

Compliment your wife every day - if you know what's good for you.

You know what makes me sick? You know what makes me so angry I just wanna play spin the bottle - at the nursing home?

Yeah - me and my old lady... we got into this thing... I like to call them 'redneck compliments'.

You know what that is? That's when you compliment somebody - by insulting them. I don't know - maybe all long-time married people do this. Maybe you do it, too.

Like we were down at the Walmart last night, and there was this big old dude walking down the aisle.
I swear he must have been possessed by the ghost of Haystacks Calhoun. My old lady looks at this guy... and she nudges me and goes... 'You didn't let yourself go *that* bad, Earl.'

Well - thank you Pearl. So what is any respectable husband supposed to do when he receives a loving compliment like that? Of course, I had to compliment her back. So I looked around... an' I go... 'See that flat-chested girl over there? At least you got just enough to hold up your tube-top, sweetheart. Even if they aren't up where they used to be.'

Then later last night, she's watching Honey Boo-Boo... and ol' Mama June did something that only makes sense to in-bred trailer trash. I watched it for a minute... shook my head and I go... 'At least you're not that stupid.'

She goes, 'Where you going?' I says, 'I'm going down to the Duck Inn and hang out. Me and the boys like to talk over the issues of the day.' And she goes, 'Yeah - in that group...you probably sound like Einstein.'

I go, 'Pearl, darlin' - you are the love of my life.' She goes, 'Thank you Earl.' And I go... 'And my life sucks.'

Wake up, America! Man Rule #17- If you're going to compliment your spouse - compliment them until it hurts. And that, ladies and gentlemen - is the secret to a long and happy marriage. I'm Earl Pitts, American. Pitts Off!

'It dawned on my last night - we're the family - other families point at in Walmart.
That's not good.'

MAN RULE # 3

The man holds the remote.

You know what makes me sick? You know what makes me so mad I just wanna hang around a dairy barn... wearing a Speedo made out of fly paper?

Here's a question I was thinking last night. How come people get buried in the coffin - clutching a Bible? It dawns on me - when you get dead, you're going to one of two places. If you go to heaven - chances are they got a full supply of the Good Book already up there. It's still the number one best seller in Heaven.

And if you're going the other direction - they're probably going to confiscate it when you go through security. Yeah - there's two places where they take away your Good Book when you enter. Hell... and Saudi Arabia.

But that's not what today's commentating is about. No sir... it ain't the Good Book. I come in the living room last night and caught my old lady clutching something else. Yeah - I come in there - and she was watching TV - holding the remote.

Women don't *HOLD* the remote. That's a guy thing. There is nothing more pathetic that seeing a woman holding a TV remote. That's like seeing a man holding a steam iron or a toilet brush. I mean - it's physically possible... but to what end? Just because we're holding it - doen't mean we know how to operate it.

There is not a woman alive that can click through channels with the speed, efficiency and professionalism of a man. Not even your BLT&G women. Number one - they slow down at all the wrong channels. Nobody slows down for Lifetime Channel or Food Channel. You slow down for ESPN... big time wrassling... or bull riding.

Yeah - and if there's a man in the room... and a woman slows down her clicking to see what they're selling on QVC - that right there is grounds for your marry-tile separation. I believe I saw that once on Matlock.

I had to gently take the remote from her hand. I said, 'Darlin' - I don't trust you with the remote. And to be fair - you shouldn't trust me either - with the laundry.

Wake up, America! Man Rule #3 - Finding your old lady holding a television remote - is like finding a three-year old holding a lit match. Act quickly - and nobody has to get hurt. I'm Earl Pitts, American. Pitts Off.

MAN RULE # 67

Sometimes woman use science to set us up.

You know what makes me sick? You know what makes me so mad I just wanna take my Swiffer Wet Jet and shove it down the throat of the next guy that calls me 'whipped'?

Some bonehead, four-eyed Pointdexter science geeks somewhere did a study a while back. And according to these lame-brain geniuses-they found the number one sex turn-on for your women. What about a guy will drive a woman wild with desire. And I know what you're thinking - it's probably those rock-hard abs of steel? Nope. Or that flowing hair like that Fabio? Nope. Fancy car - no. A ton of money - no.

What really turns on your woman of today - is the sight of a man cleaning the house. Obviously - I am suspicious about who did this research. I would not be surprised to find out it was funded - by women.

First of all... if the sight of a man pushing a mop drove women up the wall with desire - how come your People magazine 'Sexist Man Alive' is never a janitor? That kind of shoots a hole in their theory right there.

So anyways - last weekend... I thought I would test out this deal - so I started helping my old lady clean. First thing I found out - housework foreplay is a lot tougher than it sounds.

First I started Scrubble Bubblin' the bath tub. And my old lady was standing behind me... going, 'Harder, Earl! Work ik harder, Earl...!' I was Toilet Duckin' under the rim of the toilet bowl... and she was going, 'Move it faster, Earl! Move it faster!!'

I was Windexin' the picture window... and she's behind me again. 'Lower, Earl. Yes, lower... lower... oh, oooh... that's the spot!!' And then when I was cleaning the oven, she's standing there going, 'Faster, Earl... faster, faster, faster... YES!!!'

I went to vacuum the rug and I couldn't find her. She was out in the backyard smoking a cigarette. Apparently she got done cleaning before me.

Wake up, America! Man Rule #67- If you want some good lovin'... you got to start with good oven.
I'm Earl Pitts, American. Pitts Off!

'I was always told the reason women have smaller feet
- is so they can
stand closer to the kitchen sink. Who am I to argue
with evolution?'

MAN RULE # 96

Dress up for church

You know what makes me sick? You know what makes me so mad I just wanna stock the preacher's baptism tub with trout - and run a play-lake on weekdays?

Yeah - today we got a serious church issue to discuss. On account of I saw this story on the Internet computer thing. This preacher was complaining... people dress too sloppy for church.

Yeah - maybe this is in your church, too. He says in the old days - people used to get dressed up on Sundays. Guys would wear suits and ties - or at least shirts and ties. Women would wear dresses.   The kids would all be scrubbed clean. You could take the skankiest family in the neighborhood...and on Sunday's....they looked like the royal family. In fact - in the old days - people actually had something called 'church clothes'. And it was always the best clothes they owned.

He says in today's church - anything goes. People are in there in t-shirts and flip-flops! Some people even go to church in shorts. Kids are in there with their soccer and little league uniforms on.   He says there's something wrong when people can't get dressed up to spend two hours a week with God.

Now - I have heard this argument two ways. I have heard that the almighty deserves a little respect. That preparing for church is a little like preparing for heaven   It don't hurt to make a good impression for the hereafter ...in the right here now.

I have also heard...God don't care what you look like. Justas long as you're there. That the almighty judges your heart an' your soul - not your shirt an' your pants.

I remember I had an Uncle die one time and my aunt buried him in a flannel shirt an' jeans. My mama went nuts. She's telling her sister - you got to send that man to the Lord in a suit and tie. Show some respect!! And my aunt says...'If Billy went to the Pearly Gates in a suit and a tie...the Lord wouldn't know who he was.' Apparently the Good Lord is not good with faces!!

So on this very delicate question - I do not have an answer. I understand both sides. But I can tell you one thing - if my old lady dresses me up to bury me...I want her to include a name tag and my wallet. In case I have to present ID.

Wake up, America! Man Rule # 96 In our house - we get dressed up for church. Not because we fear God...we fear the wrath of my old lady. She would smote us in a heartbeat. I'm Earl Pitts, American. Pitts Off!

When two vehicles pull up to a four-way stop at
the same time -
the person who goes first is the guy with the
bigger truck
No exceptions!

Never get in line behind a fat guy at the Golden
Corral Buffet.
Life is too short.

The only acceptable guy pets are dogs.
And some large snakes.

If you're a guy and you have more than three
pairs of shoes -
what the hell's wrong with you?

MAN RULE # 38

Real men don't hike.

You know what makes me sick? You know what makes me so mad I just wanna play hacky-sack...with a live squirrel?

Yeah - my old lady watches them animal shows on the TV - and they make her stupid. Listen to this- she came up with an idea for last weekend. She says - we're going down to the state park - and we're gonna go hiking. She wants to see animals in their natural habitat.

Hiking is like going hunting - without a gun. It's kind of stupid - and it's not something rednecks will generally do. Why do you want to be in the woods - if you can't kill nothing?

Here's my theory. If you're hiking, and you see two rednecks heading down the trail in the other direction - they're headed either to a pot farm... a still... or a secret fishing hole. Because they ain't out there for no hiking.

I've always said -if the good Lord had meant for man to hike - he would never have created the all-terrain vehicle.

But we went hiking anyway. Saturday morning - bright an early. Mrs. Daniel Boone and me drove out to Mudd Lake. And we stopped at this parking lot with a big map of different trails we could take. Now you'd think tenderfoot Pearl Pitts would have picked that half-mile loop to the duck pond and back right. No. She's wants to do the five-mile hike up to the top of Cooper Hill and back. She grabs her water bottle and fanny pack and goes, 'Come on, Earl... it will be fun!'

Okay - number one - most of the stuff on earth that can actually eat a human - lives in the woods. That would include your bears... your mountain lions...your wolves... and your Sasquatches. Yeah - nothing could be more fun - than being eaten alive... by a creature most people don't believe exists.

Yeah - we had a blast. Great exercise too. Except we came back and I was loaded with bug bites... stubbed my toe on a rock...tripped over a tree root and wrenched my knee... did a running two mile battle with a yellow-jacket.. fell off a small cliff... broke a shoe lace... ran out of water... stepped on a snake. And I don't know how I did this... but I got poison ivy in my armpit. Yeah - nature is your friend. If your friend was trying to kill you.

Wake up, America! Man Rule # 38   The next time your old lady tells you she wants to take a hike - tell her she can. End of story. I'm Earl Pitts, American. Pitts Off!

MAN RULE # 321

Never replace anything that you can 'kind of' still fix.

You know what makes me sick? You know what makes me so mad I just wanna scratch my head - with a garden weasel?

Yeah - I got to get me a new yard tractor this year. The old one finally gave up the ghost. Hell - I can't believe it lasted as long as it did. Figuring me and my little boy, Earl Junior pieced it together with extra parts we found down at Ernie's Mower Fix-It Shop.

It was kind of what you call a high-breed. Except my little boy called it a Frankenstein mower. Officially - we called it the Crafty Snappy Lawn Cadet. And that sucker lasted ten years, too. It ran like a top. I mean - maybe it cut a little uneven - but that was only because one of the back tires was smaller.

But I loved that lawn mower.

And yeah - maybe if you ran the thing too long....you'd find an oil sheen on a couple passes of the grass. And every now and then the steering pin in the front fell off....and the right tire would turn right....and the left tire would turn left...and you'd have to finish the yard skidding and hopping.

But I loved that lawn mower.

And yeah - every now and then - the left blade had a tendency the work loose in the middle of cutting the grass....and Frisbee across the yard like an ankle-high Chinese death star. But it wasn't like anybody ever got hurt. And yeah - sometimes when you turned the key - you'd get a small electrical shock. And a couple times the brake pedal fell off in the middle of the yard....and I had to run the dang thing into the side of the house to get it to stop moving.

But l loved that lawn mower.

Yeah - I loved that mower. It was the worst grass cutting machine ever conceived. But me and my boy built it ourselves....and it was free. Now I got to shell out nine-hundred bucks for some panty-waist stupid Yuppie lawn mower. I wonder if Ernie's got some more parts down at his place.

Wake up, America! Man Rule # 321 - That's why they say nothing runs like a Deere. Because whatever me and my little boy piece together....it ain't gonna run nothing like a Deere. I'm Earl Pitts, American. Pitts Off!

MAN RULE # 28

Real men don't 'decorate' their yards.

You know what makes me sick? You know what makes me so mad I just wanna suck the wax out of my ear-holes and donate it to a homeless surfer? So he can wax his board, dude!

Yeah - today I want to discuss my latest research. That's right - every day you hear where some lab-coat wearin', four-eyed science dweebs were doing some kind of study or something. And they're always announcing their important results.

So I figured - what the hell -I can play that game, too. And that's how come I have spent the last two weeks figuring out the difference between a 'man yard'....and a 'woman yard'.

See - I was driving out where we live when it came to me - of all those houses you pass out there....some of them are where a guy lives alone. More than likely - his old lady took off and stuck him with the mortgage. She probably throw'd the kids in the car and hasn't been back since who knows when. So how can you tell where that guy lives.. without actually seeing...*that guy??* That's where your 'man yard' comes in.

Number one - there ain't gonna be nothing in that yard....with mulch around it. Because mulch is a woman thing. Oh - they'll use men to haul it, shovel it and pat it down ....but it's only there because a woman is present.

The number two scientifical tip-off is- the length of the grass in the yard. A man living by his lonesome will cut the grass just often enough to keep the county off his butt. And you can totally forget the tough spots...like the ditch an' around the trees. Those places are going back to nature.

Number three - the total absence of what I like to call - festive redneck yard adornment. Yeah - there ain't gonna be no chrome balls....bird fountains...dressed up cement geese...cut-out shadow people...pink flamingos....or other colorful plastic animals in the yard. Because with women...it's like they don't got enough knick-knacks *IN* the house...they got to start a collection outside. Guys don't do that.

Wake up, America! Man Rule # 28 - Here's the best way to tell if a guy lives in a house alone. Basically - if the place looks abandoned. You've heard of a bachelor pad? That's a bachelor yard. I'm Earl Pitts, American - Pitts Off!

'It's a 'front-yard' or a 'back-yard'. Real men don't have 'lawns'.

MAN RULE # 401

Men don't 'do' yard sales

You know what makes me sick? You know what makes me so mad I just wanna spank a badger?

Yeah - I took a drive with my old lady this weekend - and I was reminded of one of the biggest differences between men and women. Women like yard sales.

Now - you average red-blooded, God-fearing American man - he would rather get stuck between two elephants getting frisky - then go pawing around some other person's junk. Because that's what a yard sale is. That's people that are going to throw stuff out...and think, 'Wait - maybe I can find a sucker to buy this crap first...'

And if they live anywhere within driving distance of my old lady - it's a wise decision.

This month out in our neck of the woods - you can't drive a half mile without passing fifteen yard sales. And most of the stuff people are selling...is the stuff they picked up in other yard sales. It's like our town is playing 'hot potato' - with crap. It's the redneck circle of life!!

And now - according to my old lady - there is different yard sale shopping strategies. Like my old lady...she likes to hit them early in the morning - when the best stuff is still available. We stopped at this one sale last Saturday...the yard was still wet with dew. The Mr. and

Mrs. were there under the tree was still on their first cups of coffee. And Pearl goes, 'Earl...they'll be anxious to make their first sale...'.

Yeah - she picked up a Captain and Tenille cassette and a Kerplunk! game that was missing all its marbles. Which I thought was oddly appropriate for her.

Now me - I got to develop my own yard sale strategy. I mean, besides my current one - which is to avoid them at all cost. So here's my thinking - I go the last hour...of the last day of the yard sale. I don't even look at what's left...I just go up to the owner and offer ten bucks for everything they got left. And then I see if I scored.

Wake up, America!! Man Rule # 401 - I don't know what's more embarrassing for a real man. Digging through someone else's crap. Or sitting there in a lawn chair - hoping some hard-up loser buys yours. It might be best to avoid the situation either way. I'm Earl Pitts, American. Pitts Off!

'Obviously - a flea-market is totally different. That's like a Walmart of yard sales.'

MAN RULE # 19

We can love them and respect them - but real men don't have 'lady friends'.

You know what makes me sick? You know what makes me so mad I just wanna make a wish...and snap a wishbone with my old lady? While it's still inside a live chicken!!

You know - people are all the time asking me for my advice. Partly because I'm a beer-tender and behind the bar - it's hard to get away from people.   And partly because I am widely regarded as a genius.

But mostly because I'm stuck behind the bar.

Anyways there was this guy in the Duck Inn the other night...and he was saying it's a scientific fact that a man cannot be best friends with a woman. He says on account of - sooner or later they will become sexually, romantically and hanky-panky attracted to each other. And that gets in the way of a good friendship.

You know - I was thinking. I do not have any women friends. And I like it that way. But it ain't because I'm worried about getting turned on by a friend. Something - I might add - I do not have to worry about with Dub Meeker.

No - there are a lot of reasons I like not having woman friends. And don't get me wrong - I love women. I adore women. I worship women. I just don't want to hang out with them.

Number one - I don't want to look at pictures. Baby pictures, prom pictures, vacation pictures. Women love to show pictures. Men hate to look at them. This way - I don't got to hurt nobody's feelings.

Number two - I don't have to set there listening to some woman yammering away about every kid, husband, parent, uncle, aunt, neighbor, in-law this side of death. I don't got to pretend to listen. And I don't got to pretend to care.

Number three - I don't got to go shopping. I don't got to go to any chick flicks. I don't got to go to the bathroom with another human being. I don't got to go to Zumba class or through a salad bar. And I sure as hell don't got to sit on a phone three hours a night going, 'Uh huh.....Uh huh.....Uh huh....'

Wake up, America! Man Rule #19 - If you don't have a lady friend - you'll never get invited to a baby shower....or a bridal shower. If you don't have a lady friend - technically - you don't even have to 'take' a shower. I'm Earl Pitts, American. Pitts Off!

MAN RULE # 67

There are 400 buttons on your remote. You need to know five of them.

You know what makes me sick? You know what makes me so mad I just wanna get into a butt-kicking contest - with a one-legged man? Yeah - that's not only mad - it's kind of cruel, too.

Here's how you can tell you're getting older. One day you wake up - and you want less buttons to push. Simple enough right? Easy and uncomplicated. It dawns on you that the Good Lord put you on this earth with one button - that being your belly-button. And that's kind of how you'd like to go out.

 The problem is - the world is moving to more buttons. I mean - even down at the plant. I worked a machine for ten years, it had three buttons and a foot pedal. Then they put in this computer deal… it was like operating a nuclear power plant. The only difference was - two days into it - I was the one that melted down.

That's when they put me on the tow motor… and I never looked back.

Here's another example… I'm looking at my TV remote right now. Look at this thing? People - I want to work a TV - not a dad-gum space shuttle!!

Here's what your TV clicker needs... on and off... sound up or down... and channel up or down. I had this remote for six years - there's still buttons on here - I don't know what they do. Like here's a button - 'menu'. Can you order food on your TV? Doesn't that seem a little bit extravagant?

Then you got 'guide', 'select', 'aspect', 'source'. I got buttons on here for 'day' and 'page'. Apparently not only does this gizmo work the TV... it works a book, too.

Did you ever hit the wrong button on your TV remote and something popped up on your screen there - and you couldn't get it off? Yeah - I had some cockamamie display on my TV once for two days. I couldn't get it off. Finally I gave up - and bought a new TV.

Wake up, America! Man Rule # 67 - If it's got a instruction book to tell you how to work all the buttons - there's too many buttons. That's how come I don't got a smart phone. I ain't that smart. But I gotta go. My old lady called - and she can't turn on the TV - I got the remote. I'm Earl Pitts, American. Pitts Off.

'I like simple stuff with one button. Those items would include your garage remote - and I'm guessing your nuclear football.'

MAN RULE # 254

Embrace your routine

You know what makes me sick? You know what makes me so mad I just wanna rip the linoleum off a bus-terminal bathroom floor - *with my teeth??!*

Let me say this - over the years - men have been conditioned to take a lot of crap. You notice whenever there's a war - they don't send the women and children. When the boat is sinking and they're manning the lifeboats - who do they call to get in first? Not the men.

We get it, okay.

Here's the only thing any man worth his salt wants out of life. A good routine. Ladies - we are simple animals. We figure out the fastest, cheapest, easiest way to get through life - and we're good.   And I mean - we're good - every day for the rest of our lives.

Like my old lady says to me last night - she goes, 'Earl... you do the same thing the same way every day. You get up... go to the same old job... come home... go to work at the same old bar... come home... go to bed.' And I add... '...with the same old woman...' She ignores that and she says, 'Earl - you are in a rut, son. Don't you ever wanna change up your life? Don't you ever want to shake things up?"

That's stupid talk. It took me over 40 years to get this down. It's like if you watch the movie Shawshank Redemption with your old lady. That movie's over - and a woman will go... 'I can't believe that old boy dug a hole through a brick wall with a spoon... and it took him 10 years.' Men don't just believe it. We're doing it!!

Yeah - that's what you call your megaphone for a man's life. We're just trying to get to the other side of life... one spoonful of crap at a time!

In fact - what you ladies call, 'shaking things up.'... men consider 'messing things up.' We drink the same morning coffee out of the same coffee cup... go to the same job... come home to our same families... and watch our same shows. And I submit to you women - that is not a rut. That is life. And we like it. And that's all your man needs to keep him happy. Until the boat starts to sink.

Wake up, America! Man Rule # 254 - When a man tries to do something different - when he tries to shake things up - that's usually when he ends up on COPS. Keep it simple - keep it routine. I'm Earl Pitts, American. Pitts Off.

**'My old lady says I'm set in my ways. I like to think -
I finally figured it out.'**

Never buy a vehicle so big that you can't
reach around to smack a kid.

If you use WD-40 to un-stick Duct Tape -
It's like watching Batman fight Spiderman.

Every now and then - you need to climb a tree -
without shooting something.

Relax. If they really wanted you to stop -
they would have put a light there.

MAN RULE # 35

A real man cherishes his socks.

You know what makes me sick? You know what makes me so mad I just wanna take those Fruit of the Loom boys down to the zoo - and throw them to the monkeys?

You know what doesn't get any credit... no thank you... and no fan-fare in this world today? And I mean besides your every-day, hard-working, flag-waving, red-blooded American.

Here's what I'm thinking. Socks.

To be more precise - the official foot-gear of the American Redneck - the white sock. Now - I was thinking on this because my old lady just bought me a bag of new white socks.

And let me tell you something. When a redneck slips on a new white sock for the first time... he knows what it must feel like when a newlywed bride slips on her first nightie. The anticipation... the fabric sliding against the skin... the goose-bumps... the quickening of the heart. And remember - this is just putting on a sock! I love a good pair of socks.

That's how come I can never understand when I see them brain-dead Yuppie idiots walking around in shoes with naked feet in them. They say -'Iit's too hot for socks,

Earl.' Yeah - well - it's too hot for underpants, too... but I'm still wearing them.

That's what it is - socks are underpants for your feet. And no real American man is walking around foot commando.

Now to the question - how come redneck socks have to be white? Number one - easier to clean. You don't got to pull a load out of the dryer - and start matching up colors. Because white socks - all match. Fact is - you know how people all complain about the dryer eating their socks... they're always missing a sock?? If all you got is white socks - you'd never know. Until you were down to one.

Think of the time that would save you each year - looking for lost socks.

The other question - the answer - mid-calf length. Knee socks if you're on a softball team... ankle length if you're on a yacht. Everybody else - standard issue.

Wake up, America! Man Rule # 35 - Your mama used to tell you to wear clean underpants - in case you were in an accident. That goes double for socks. I'm Earl Pitts, American. Pitts Off!

MAN RULE # 17

Respect other people's rules - even if it means putting on a shirt and shoes.

You know what makes me sick? You know what makes me so mad I just wanna spank a bobcat?

Yeah - me and my business partner, Pete the bartender - we made a little executive business decision last night. And this was on account of that stupid sign he put on the front door of the Duck Inn.

Now the sign says... 'No Shirt - No Shoes - No Service'. He thinks that keeps out the riff-raff, the low-life and the undesirable elements of the neighborhood. I think it hurts business.

I explained to Pete last night. I says, "Pete - what if some old boy out there won the lottery... and had a million dollars in his pocket? And what if he wanted to come in here and wanted to blow every penny on buying drinks for everybody in the bar? But what if somehow in all the excitement... he had lost his shoes? Should we turn that man away at the door?' He nods his head and he goes, 'You got a point, Earl.'

And I go, 'And what if a country music superstar touring bus pulls up outside - and Faith Hill or Sara Evans run in here for a quick beer. *But* - they had forgot to put their shirts on? Should we turn them away at the door?' He nods his head and goes, 'Another excellent point, Earl.' He says. 'I was more thinking about Dub Meeker without a shirt on. I never considered Sara Evans.'

I says - 'What if Faith Hill wanted to come in here - and she didn't have a shirt on... *or shoes?*' He goes, 'Earl - I would take the door off the hinges!'

So we replaced our door sign last night - because you never know when a lottery winner or a naked female singing superstar wants to come in your bar. It now says - No Yuppies. No Little Yappy Dogs. Nobody hoping to find Dixie Chicks on the jukebox. No Pinkos. No ACLU or PETA types. Nobody in bicycle pants. And definitely - Nobody that wants us to turn on the soccer game.

Except at one point - Pete goes, 'Earl - what if Sara Evans come in here without a shirt on and wanted us to turn on the soccer game?' I go,' Pete... now you're way over-thinking this.'

Wake up, America! Man Rule # 17 - Walking into a redneck bar is like getting into heaven. We don't care what you look like. We're just glad you're here. I'm Earl Pitts, American. Pitts Off.

'No shirt - No shoes - No service might be a smart business call - but it does discriminate against nudists. And having seen some of these people - I don't want them outside picketing.'

MAN RULE # 9

If you're an idiot - don't blame anybody else.

You know what makes me sick? You know what makes me so mad I just wanna host a wet T-shirt contest - at the old folks home? Yikes!!

I hate it when people do something evil... or stupid... or sad. And then instead of other people calling that person evil or a dummy. They say, 'Well - he had a bad childhood.'

Here's what I think. Do you know when you can blame your poor childhood for your actions? Yeah - when you're a child!!

I don't need no pointy-headed, psycho Dr. Phil wannabes coming up with excuses for you being the sorry idiot you are. You know, when some evil loner takes out half of his workplace with a arsenal of semi-automatic weapons... did any of you psycho-babble, twisted geniuses ever stop to think - maybe he was just having a bad adulthood?

Nope. It was because Rambo there was emotionally scarred as a child. His mama did not breast feed him. His daddy was distant and aloof. I don't even know what the hell 'aloof' means. Except - it's a 'fool' spelled backwards. Which seems appropriate. Because that's exactly what you people are - when you try to come up with excuses for evil.

Hey - I don't know a lot of people who had childhoods like Richie Rich or Little Orphan Annie... (after the adoption, of course). No sir. Most of us come from humble, real-American families... where we grew up with our share of struggle, turmoil and grief. That doesn't mean we're all wound so tight - the next time anybody looks at us funny - we got the right to snap.

I'm thinking if everybody that ever had a bad childhood got a free pass for being evil this wouldn't be life - this would be a Mad Max movie. And we'd all be in the Thunderdome right now. But we're not. And do you know how come? Because 99.9% of us got the where with all to suck it up, put on our big-boy pants - and get on with life.

Wake up, America!   Man Rule # 9 - There's only two acceptable reasons how come people do bad things. Because they're evil. Or because they're on drugs. Leave their struggle with potty training out of it.   I'm Earl Pitts, American. Pitts Off.

'If you think it's a big deal because you weren't loved
as a child - I got news for you.
We don't like you now either.

MAN RULE # 182

Real men don't eat kiwi.

You know what makes me sick? You know what makes me so mad I just wanna force the Chiquita Banana Lady to dance - on Monkey Island? Yeah - let's see how far she gets with a head full of fruit.

Here's another reason how come I love summer. It's your chance to eat fresh fruit. I sincerely believe if you think back to the top ten happiest moments in your life - at least six of them will involve eating watermelon.

And while I am definitely NOT one a' them holier-than-thou, stuck-up, food Nazis, the fact is - fresh fruit is good for you. It don't make you fat. It keeps the pipes clean. And it keeps your ticker happy.

That being said - I think that it's important that we all realize- there's guy fruit. And there's woman fruit.

For a sample... a banana is a perfect man fruit. Of course - you don't want to look your buddy in the eye when you're eating one. That is an awkward moment. But bananas are guy fruit. Guy fruit would be bananas, apples, oranges... and watermelon. Simple - basic, God Bless America... fruit.

Of course - us men will eat other fruit - as long as it's baked in a pie. Blueberry pie, blackberry pie, cherry pie... lemon pie... huckleberry pie.

Now you woman fruit - tends to be in the melon family. Cantaloupes and Honeydews. And they like them little freaky fruits… tangerines… tanger-ellos. Nectarines… necta-rellos. Plums.. plum-erellos. You ever seen these things called 'kiwis'? They look like cactus testicles. Woman love them things. They shouldn't call them things 'kiwis'. They should call them 'desert oysters'.

Then of course you got your fruit enjoyed by men and women equally. Or what I like to call - your bisexual fruit. Peaches. Everybody loves peaches. Peach cobbler, peach pie, peach Danish. Peach on earth - goodwill toward men. That's what I say.

Wake up, America! Man Rule # 182 - If you ever see a man eating a kiwi - take away his man card. If you ever see a woman eating a banana - lucky you. I'm Earl Pitts. Pitts Off.

**'The most deceptively named food ever -
is fruit cocktail.
I had three last night - and didn't feel anything!!'**

MAN RULE # 173

Real Men don't shop.

You know what makes me sick? You know what makes me so mad I just wanna go on Amazon and go nuts? And I don't mean America's favorite shopping web site... I mean the actual river!!

Runt Wilson's brother, Woody came in the Duck Inn last night... and let me tell you something - he looked like the cat that just ate the canary. I mean he marches in there like a county politician at a pancake breakfast.

He sets down at the bar - and he goes - 'Earl, you are a fraud, son.' He goes, 'I got you dead to rights.' And I go - 'What are you talking about?'

And he says... 'Me and my old lady seen you down at the Walmart last night. And I don't know how many times I have head you say - you have never went shopping a day in your life.' He says, 'I caught you shopping, Earl - you big fraud.'

Okay - so let's straighten some points out here. Your actual red-blooded, real American male - does not go shopping. We go - *buying*. So if you caught me in the Walmart - I wasn't shopping. I was buying.

Now you woman of the species - shops. They like to go in stores to look at stuff they *could* buy. Then they consider stuff *might* buy. And then they try it on to see if it's stuff they *should* buy. And that's just the beginning. Then - they spend a lot of time looking around to see if there's something else - they should buy instead.

Your real man ain't got the time, the inclination or the genetic make-up for such nonsense. He already knows what he needs when he walks in the store. So he goes in - and gets it. That ain't 'shopping'. That's 'getting'.

In fact - a man will say, 'I got to go down to the store and 'get' some smokes.' Or - 'I got to go 'get' milk.' A woman says - 'I'm going shopping.' They like to spend money - but they just don't 'get' it. Yeah - and when a woman 'goes shopping' - the only thing she 'gets' - is distracted... confused... and way behind on her credit card balance. That don't sound like something we're interested in.

Wake Up, America! Man Rule #173 - That's the three 'gets' when a man goes in a store. Get in. Get what you're looking for. And get the hell out. I'm Earl Pitts, American. Pitts Off.

'If you can find you a woman that hates to go shopping - that woman is a keeper. And I don't care if she looks like Barney Fife.'

MAN RULE # 58

Big words don't scare us. Even if we don't know what they mean.

You know what makes me sick? You know what makes me so mad I just wanna juggle electric eels?

I just wanna give you all a sample of the brain-power I hang around with every night down at the Duck Inn. It's not like it's the nightly meeting of MENSA. Hell - the boys down there wouldn't qualify for the high IQ club - if you added all their IQ's together.

Of course - being dim-witted never stopped a redneck from a challenge. So okay - last night there's this new guy comes in the bar. He's kind of quiet. You know - maybe a little bookish... or metrosexual for the Duck Inn, let's say. But we don't discriminate. An' we got the game on. So Junior Meeker tries to start up a conversation with this guy. I mean - if you're gonna be in there - you're gonna be in the family - so to speak.

Junior goes... 'Who you rooting for, buddy?' The guy looks at Junior and he goes - 'I am ambivalent.' Well - Junior looks stumped at first. Then a light-bulb goes off in his little idiot head and he crinkles up his face and goes... 'Are you telling me you can breathe under water??'

And the guy goes - 'No, that's amphibious.' Junior goes…
'Whoa - you can write with either hand?' The guy looks
at Junior like you might look at one of those crusty-eyed
puppies in the Human Society commercials. It's a
combination of pity - and disbelief. The guy goes…
'No... that's ambidextrous' And Junior pinches up his
face again… and goes… 'Ambidextrous? Ain't that
where you date boys *and* girls… and you don't care
which one?' And the guy goes, 'No - that would be
bisexual.'

And Junior goes… 'Well, why didn't you just say so.
Listen buddy - if you're bisexual - it don't make no
difference to us. We don't discriminate. Course we don't
want to date you or nothing, neither.

At this point - the guy's getting frustrated. He says, 'I am
not bisexual! You asked me a question about a game. I
was merely telling you my feelings for either team. I am
ambiguous!

And Junior sets back and says… 'There you go -
breathing underwater again.

Wake up, America! Man Rule #58 - Never let knowledge
and a command of the language get in the way of a good
argument. Besides - everybody knows ambiguous is
when you got more than one wife. Idiots. I'm Earl Pitts,
American. Pitts Off.

MAN RULE # 8

Dogs and cats are not your kids.

You know what makes me sick? You know what makes me so mad I just wanna go down to the park wearing a pair of rubber gloves - and offer to pick up other people's dog poop?

What can I tell you - I'm a helpful kind of guy.

Here's the deal - I have a brand new pet peeve. I think you all know my biggest pet peeve of all time. That's when some poor backward idiot drives a roofing nail through his forehead with a nail-gun - the doctors yank it out - the guy survives... and the doctors say - 'He was very lucky.'

I would submit to you - the 'very lucky' among us - have not shot nails into our brains. The 'very lucky' scratch off $100 instant tickets. They are not spackling their foreheads.

So that's my number one pet peeve. Here's my new number two. Pet parents. Have y'all seen these dog food and cat food commercials where people call themselves - 'pet parents'?

I got news for you people. If you did not give birth on a dirty blanket in the back of the closet - you are not a pet parent. If you did not lick the schmutz off of the head of your baby when it was born - you are not a pet parent. If you did not lay on your side and let a half dozen newborns suckle from your impressive array of nipples - you are not a pet parent.

So let's get this straight. You 'own' dogs and cats. You are the 'parent' - of little baby humans. And I know it gets confusing sometimes. You can go down to the park tomorrow- and you might see people with dogs wearing sweaters. And little kids - on leashes. And you're thinking - what the hell is going on?? Is this person near-sighted or what??? Didn't he notice which one had fur?

It's simple - if you got a dog - you 'own' a dog. It's a dog. I do not want to attend it's birthday party - and I do not want to see its name on the bottom of your Christmas card. I do not want to see pictures of it on your phone. Why? Because it's a dog.

Wake up, America! Man Rule # 8 - Your dog might be man's best friend. But unless you can pick him up by the scruff of his neck - *with your teeth* - he is not your kid. I'm Earl Pitts, American. Pitts Off.

**'You feed them, you care for them, you keep them in your house. In those ways,
dogs might be considered a member of the family.
But kids don't chase cars
and you don't have to pretend you don't know them
when they bite somebody
down the street.'**

Never stop and ask a woman for directions.
She won't t know either.

It's okay to hug your child -
as long as you're both not male
over the age of twelve.

It's never really about the toilet seat.

If a woman says to you,
'Hey - my eyes are up here.'
Say, 'Yeah - but I don't want to
play with your eyes.'

MAN RULE # 278

If we say a fish is a 'keeper' - that's because it's dead - and tasty.

You know what makes me sick? You know what makes me so mad I just wanna try to sneak into Sea World with a peg leg... and a harpoon? Yeah - that ought to freak out Shamu.

Yeah - my little boy, Earl Junior come home the other day from a high school fund-raiser. He had a plastic bag filled with water... and there's a gold-fish swimming around in there. I says... 'What you gonna do with the fish?' He looks at the fish and he goes...I don't know - keep it.

Now - at this point, I should have jumped up... snatched the bag out of his hands... run to the toilet... and saved myself a world of heart-ache. But fact is - I don't move as fast as I used to. Cause my old lady come in there before I moved an inch.

This is a woman that's been wanting an aquarium since the day we got married. They got an actual 'guys building aquariums' show on the TV - and she's hooked on it. (get it?) She has been begging me for twenty-some years to buy her an aquarium. I am personally opposed. I think being a fisherman with an aquarium... is like being a hunter raising baby deer in the garage. There's just something fundamentally wrong with it.

Here's the problem with having a aquarium. Number one - you have to go to the aquarium store. Who has ever gone into a aquarium store... took a good whiff and thought... 'Man, I'd like that smell in *my* house.'

Plus - the people you will find at an aquarium store are just a tad more creepy than the people you will find lined up at the methadone clinic. It is not a hobby that attracts normal people.

Number two... that free goldfish you won with the ping-pong ball at the spring social - will end up costing over three hundred bucks - if you want to do it right. And my old lady insists we want to do it right. Yeah - the way I see it - if we 'did it right'... Nemo would be swimming around the waste treatment plant right now.

Wake up, America! Man Rule # 278. 'In a real man's world - the only people that need to keep fish in big tanks, are Sea World... and dentists.' And honestly, I don't understand the dentist thing. I'm Earl Pitts, American. Pitts Off!

'I told my old lady, 'If that fish dies - you owe me 300-bucks for this stupid aquarium.'
He's still alive. Although I caught her twice last night - giving him mouth-to-mouth'

MAN RULE # 39

I don't look like an Olsen twin - so don't expect me to eat like one.

You know what makes me sick? You know what makes me so mad I just wanna practice tying rattlesnakes into knots?

Yeah - me and the Meeker boys did something funny last weekend. Junior was telling up his old lady found a new restaurant downtown. And he says from what she was saying - we ought to go try it out.

Dub Meeker goes, 'What's the big deal about that?' And Junior goes, 'Get this - the place is run by women… and they put their menu on a giant black-board with colored chalk.' Well - you know what that means, right? This place is either run by health food nuts - or lesbitarians.

So we go to this place. And I'll tell you right now - it ain't your Denny's. We grab a table and pretty soon this woman come up to us… got that Bob Marley hair-do and a nose-ring. And she goes, 'Hello gentlemen. Would you like to know what our specials are today?' And Dub goes, 'Sister, we're always hungry.'

And she goes, 'Well, we got two menus - we have a low-sodium, gluten-free, organic menu with no trans-fat - featuring free-range chicken raised with no antibiotics or steroids. Our beef cattle lead a carefree life eating flowers in a mountain meadow and then softly lulled to sleep by a Swiss yodeler... before being humanely slaughtered.

We also have a vegan menu featuring unprocessed, conflict-free whole grains, and community-supported and nutrient-dense fruits and vegetables from sustainable farming practices certified non-GMO. Then we're also featuring fair-trade coffee served with almond or soy milk and served by a barista making a living wage.'

We all looked at each other... and Dub whispers under his breath to me... Earl - I think you're right. They're lesbitarians.'

Junior goes, 'I hope you don't use MSG - I'm allergic to MSG.' And the girl scrunches up her face and goes - 'Dang It! We missed one.' Yeah - we couldn't eat there - it was unhealthy.

Wake up, America! Man Rule # 39. - It seems to me - if you free-range your animals before you kill them... making them feel happy and content. That just makes it all the meaner. You're tricking them.
I'm Earl Pitts, American. Pitts Off.

**'Don't be fooled by your waitress's purple hair and all the metal sticking out of her face.
That doesn't necessarily mean the food's
going to be good.'**

MAN RULE # 52

**Tell small children not to run with scissors.
Everything else is open game.**

You know what makes me sick? You know what makes me so mad I just wanna go in a cave with a stick... and wake up bats?

Today - I wanna talk to you about something in this country that has just gone over the top. You know how when those touchy-feely, liberal, yuppie pinheads get hold of something - and just over think it? Yeah - I think they're killing childhood.

Childhood is supposed to a good thing. At least it was when we were kids. That was fun times. You'd spend 16 hours a day playing... and the rest sleeping. You'd be climbing trees... riding your bike all over God's creations... baseball... football... you'd play army... and you knew every inch of your neighborhood.

Today - apparently childhood is too dangerous for our kids. Like Runt Wilson was telling me last night down at the Duck Inn... he went over to his daughter's house but his granddaughter wasn't there - on account of his daughter said she was on a 'play date' with a little girl down the street. Yeah - today parents arrange 'play dates'.

You know how we arranged to play when we was kids? We went outside! Yeah - and we played. Because there was other kids out there, too!!

And I'll tell you another thing. Every time we stepped out of the house when we were kids - we weren't wearing some stupid helmet. Call us dare-devil rebels - but back in those days a kid was expected to get knocked silly a couple times. Because back then - it was good for you. It'd toughen up your head.

I remember I got hit in the melon by a ball-bat one time… fell off my bike a hundred times… fell out of a tree more than once… fell down the stairs a couple times… got hit in the head by a horse-shoe… took snowballs to the head… fell on ice... not one time was I wearing a helmet. And look at me today.

Okay - maybe that's a bad example.

Wake up, America! Man Rule # 52 -   Back when we were kids, you could make it through childhood by following two simple rules. Don't run with scissors... and don't play in traffic. Everything else - you were on your own.   And obviously - we're still here.   Well - the majority of us. I'm Earl Pitts, American. Pitts Off.

'I have never run with scissors. Not because my mama told me not to.
It's just I have never felt the need to cut paper while I was running.'

MAN RULE #97

Be careful what you wish for - like growing up.

You know what makes me sick? You know what makes me so mad I just wanna choke Captain Crunch... until his windpipe goes snap, crackle and pop?

Yeah - my little boy, Earl Junior was moping around the house last weekend. You know how teenagers get... kind of like a hunting dog with worms. Moving around like something's bugging them inside... but they don't know what.

Anyways - he says to me - he can't wait to be an adult - because being a kid sucks.

So I sit him down... and I go, 'Son - you're probably looking at the awesome and exciting life your old man here leads. And that might throw you off as to the true nature of being an adult.'   I says, 'Cause let me clue you in - being an adult ain't no bed of roses, neither.'

He says - 'You don't got to go to school. You don't got homework every night. You get to drive. Nobody tells you when you got to be home.'

And I go... 'Everything you say there might be true. But here's something nobody ever tells you about being an adult. Adult cereal stinks.

I says, "When I was your age… I was up to my eyeballs in Lucky Charms, Trix, Coco Crispies, Count Chocula and Fruit Loops. Every breakfast I got a sugar buzz and a toy surprise.

And you know the surprise you pull out of a box of adult cereal? The surprise is - they can even sell this stuff. It's a little biscuit of fiber that looks like they dried out something the cat coughed up. And have you ever seen a box of granola, son? It's like they sifted yard waste through a screen - and whatever fell through - they put in the box.' I says, 'When you're a kid - you choose your cereal based on the flavor and the toy surprise inside. When you're an adult - you choose your cereal based on whether you need your cholesterol lowered… or your pipes flushed out.'

Wake up, America! Man Rule # 97 - Happy Meals' got a toy surprise. Kids' cereals' got a toy surprise.
So what's surprising to me - is why any kids even want to grow up. I'm Earl Pitts, American. Pitts Off.

**'The only time an adult is 'surprised' by what's inside their food - is if they're
brand new to this country - and bite into their first corn dog.**

61

MAN RULE # 36

We can't read your mind - you have to tell us what you want.

You know what makes me sick? You know what makes me so mad I just wanna   Three Stooges eye-poke a grizzly bear?

Today - I am declaring war on the wishy-washy... the undecided... the people that don't got the guts or the fortitude to tell the rest of us what they want.

You know who I'm talking about, right? It's those mealy-mouth, time-wasting butt-wipes... every time you ask them where they wanna go... or what they wanna do... they always go, 'Oh, I don't care.'

Like last night... I took my old lady out to eat nice - down to the steak house out by the Interstate. She says, 'Earl, every single time you take me out nice... we come here.' She goes... 'How come we always got to come here?'

I says - 'Because... every time I take you out nice - I ask you where you want to go. And every time you say - 'I don't care'. And I go - 'Well, I care, Pearl. And I like steak.'

You know - if I was a mind-reader, I'd get me a crystal ball and start telling fortunes for ten bucks a pop. But unfortunately - the good Lord seen fit to short-change me in the psychic sciences - so here's a simple man rule - any time you ask somebody what they want to do… or eat.. or where they wanna go - and they tell you they don't care… here's what you do. Do something that will scare the living hell out of them.

Like if your mother-in-law is over… and she says she don't care what you watch on the TV… try slipping in a couple porn videos.

Or your old lady says she don't care where you take her to eat? Take her down to that new Chinese place where they kill the live snake at your table.

Your buddies is all jacked up after bowling… and everybody wants to keep going - but nobody cares where. I suggest Bingo.

Wake up, America! Man Rule #36 - This one's simple for all you wishy-washy, nitwit loser people. If you know what you wanna do - just tell us. And if you really don't care - shut up and eat your snake. That's hard to screw up. I'm Earl Pitts, American. Pitts Off.

'If you don't care what we do - then I don't care if you complain after we do it.'

MAN RULE # 25

Man don't have stress. We get 'worked up'.

You know what makes me sick? You know what makes me so mad I just wanna find that 'Don't Worry-Be Happy' dude... and beat the living snot out of him?

Yeah - today I want to talk about stress. With all the crap going on in the world right now - these goofy-headed brain-experts say all that stress can filter down to our personal lives. Yeah. They say we got to learn how to deal with and minimize stress.

Apparently these twisted, scientifical goobers don't have wives and kids. They must not have thankless jobs working for idiots. And they obviously don't have mortgages or bills to pay. Hey, you four-eyed science dweebs - slip off the lab coat and come visit the real world every now and then. This country has been stressed out since the 60's!

But maybe these science, Pointdexter yahoos do got a point. Maybe all of a sudden - too many of us are letting it get to us. I took a poll down at the Duck Inn... exactly one-half of my buddies are on blood pills. And the other half probably would be - if they didn't refuse to go to the doctor.

See - there's a whole bunch of stuff in a redneck's life that causes him stress. Except - out where we live - we don't call it 'stress'. We call it 'getting worked up'. And there is a never-ending list of stuff that will get a redneck worked up. His old lady. His kids. His job. His old lady's kin. His kin. His boss. His truck. His bills. Sports. Politics. PETA, women working in auto-parts stores, liberals, cell phones, metro-sexuals, evil-doers, gasoline prices, home repairs, butt-head idiot celebrities. When I just *see* Hillary Clinton or John Boehner... the veins in my neck get close to bursting.

Then you got your government pin-heads... your NSA, your IRS, your TSA, your DOJ. You find out what these evil losers are doing... and you realize you're SOL... and probably DOA.

Wake up, America! Man Rule # 25 - Whatever you call it - it can't be good. I accept the fact stress is bad... and too much stress can cut a man down in his prime. My question is - how come we ain't already dead? I'm Earl Pitts, American. Pitts Off!

**'When a rich man is stressed out - he looks to his
psychologist or his doctor.
A Redneck - gets drunk.'**

MAN RULE #217

There should be more women in politics.

You know what makes me sick? You know what makes me so mad I just wanna bonk John Boehner and Harry Reid's heads together - like they were the lesser two of the Three Stooges.

I was listening to politician commercials yesterday and I thought of something.   How come there aren't more women in politics? I know that's a little weird coming from me. On account of - running the world seems to be man-business.

But I ain't talking about the actual running the world part. I'm just talking *about* running for office. That is a job fit for a woman.

For example - you can spend up to a year trying to convince people you're always right. Now - I don't want to sound sexist - but who in your house does that?

If your opponent does something stupid - you will remember it - and bring it up every chance you get. Often times - for years. Once again - I ain't gonna say nothing - but draw your own conclusions.

You like to hold babies... check. You like to make small-talk with strangers... check. You enjoy a debate with your opponent... which is basically talking each other to death. Check. When somebody calls you up and complains about something... you have to actually pretend that you care. Wow. All these seem to be in what you call - your female wheel-house.

You spend a lot of time pointing out your opponent's short-comings... check.   Once you get in office... you can hold a grudge from now until the cows come home. Double-check.   And most people seem to think sometimes you talk... just because you like the sound of your own voice. That - ladies and gentlemen is triple-check... and checkmate!!

Come to think of it... I don't even know why guys are interested in running.

Wake up, America!   Man Rule # 217 - I don't know if Hillary Clinton will be the next President.   But I'll tell you this - she's got the right chromosomes.   Kind'a like Bruce Springsteen - she was born to run.   I'm Earl Pitts, American.   Pitts Off.

'I told my old lady I couldn't be a politician because I can't stand people, I think government is a joke and I couldn't care less what other people want. She said, "Barack Obama didn't let that stop him.'

Ferrets, weasels, marmot and de-skunked skunks
are not pets.
Never have a pet that once dead - you may get the
urge to turn it into a hat.

Never bite off more than you can chew.
Unless we're talking actual *food* - and you're a
guy - in which case it's expected of you.

If the world is ever taken over by monkeys -
don't try to escape by climbing a tree.

If your old lady gets in your face and screams,
'Are you deaf?!?' -
stare back at her blankly - like you can't hear her.

MAN RULE # 16

A chef with a nose-ring and a tattoo doesn't make it a dive.

You know what makes me sick? You know what makes me so mad I just wanna scrape off and eat anything that pops off the underside of a cafeteria table in the State Pen?

Yeah - I hate when some stuck-up, Yuppie yahoo misrepresents the redneck world. There is a big difference between claiming you're a redneck. And *being* a redneck.

Obviously - I'm talking about Guy Ferrrari… that mouth-breathing, bristle-headed idiot on the Eating Channel. He's got a show on there called *'Diners, Drive-Ups and Dives.'* Only problem is - I have never seen a dive on that show. He seems to think if he can find a place where the chef has more tattoos than a circus freak and jewelry in his nose - that makes it a dive.

That don't make it a dive.

And - you can't put a show on there - and promise rednecks you're gonna show them dives. And then not show them dives. That's what you call your falsified advertising. I remember once - he had a so-called dive on there… he said it was a remodeled gas station. I have ate in restaurants - that were *STILL* gas stations.

Sometimes you'd be eating there - and they'd ask you to move your table closer to the wall - so they could get a car in for a brake-job. I submit to you - that's a dive.

So just to be accurate - here is how you can tell your eating establishment is a dive - and not some fancy-schmancy, poupon-sucking, snail-eating, hoity-toity five-star eatery - *disguised* as a dive.

Number one - do they got a big gravel lot out back for trucks? That would be a dive. Do they got a bottle of them little green chili peppers on the table? That would be a dive.

Can you smell the restrooms - before you actually go IN the restrooms? That's a dive. Do they like to joke about disease when you're ordering? Like if you ask - how's the chili today? And they go - 'Well - nobody died from it yet this week. That we know of...' That's a dive. Your finer Yuppie establishments don't kid about food poisoning. Makes you wonder what they're hiding.

Wake up, America! Man Rule # 16 - And no matter what you order - even if you're just having a cup of coffee - do they put that squeeze bottle of ketchup on the table. Just in case. That's a dive. And I'm Earl Pitts, American. Pitts Off.

'You know that restroom cleaning check-chart on the back of the toilet door?
If the last entry on there was 1986 - that's a dive.'

71

MAN RULE # 145

Everything we used to do as kids - is better than what they do now. Everything!

You know what makes me sick? You know what makes me so mad I just wanna do a double-twisting back-flip from the pike position off the ten-meter platform - and land in a damp sponge?

Here's the thing that's got my goat - Swimming today… ain't like the swimming we done when we were kids.

I've been seeing these commercials they got on there about these big fancy new water parks. With their slides… and their splashing pools… and acres and acres of liquid fun. And they got those big new city pools and county recreational pools.

You know what we had when we were kids? A swimming hole. And I'm not trying to go all 'Andy Griffith' on you, neither. I mean, it wasn't that long ago all a kid needed to entertain himself in the summer was a pair a cut-offs - and a lake.

I mean - back when we were kids - you had two choices to get wet in the summer time. You could go down to the lake and chance the snapping turtles and water moccasins. Or, you stayed home and pulled out the Slip n' Slide. In one case, you could get drug under by a giant snapper… or lose a leg to water moccasin poison. Or at the very least pick up God knows what kind of bacteria or

flesh-eating parasite.   And before you got back in the car
- your mama would check you for leeches.

But if you stayed home… you became known as a Wuss.
So that was pretty much settled.

I mean - my old lady had my kid down to the county pool
the other day… they pulled everybody out of the water on
account of - the pH was out of balance.   I'll tell you
what… I crawled out of Mudd Lake many a time when I
was a kid… I had an actual crust on me.

So do me a favor this summer - save our children from
being known as hopeless wimps and wussies. Find
yourself a lake… or a pond… or one of your slower
moving river. And throw your kids in there. Assuming of
course - your kids can swim.

Wake up America!   Man Rule   # 145 -   If your kids
complain that fish poop in the water at the lake -
remind them - at the Splash Park… the fat kids do. I'd
take my chances with the leeches. I'm Earl Pitts,
American. Pitts Off.

MAN RULE # 92

People who fail to plan - plan to fail   Except men - we're just not that into it.

You know what makes me sick? You know what makes me so mad I just wanna smack two penguins together like I was cleaning erasers?

I know – that don't make sense – but it will be stuck in your head the rest of the day.

I just figured out another thing that makes your man and your woman of the species different. And, trust me - I'm not saying one is better than the other – just different.

Here it is - women love to plan. You go to a wedding, a birthday party, a reunion, an anniversary party, a bake sale or a funeral - basically any event where people gotta be someplace at a specific time. And I guaran-dang-tee you – it was not planned by a man. That's gonna have woman's fingerprints all over it.

That is because men are not born with with the genetical planning chromosome.   This was one of the reasons I was surprised to see gay guys getting married. Who the hell plans the dang thing?!?! If you got two straight guys together... they couldn't plan meeting for lunch right. They'd end up at different Denny's - on different days.

You ask any man to prepare and plan any event… and the best you can hope for is a cold case of beer and a topped-off tank of propane for the grill. And even then – your man will think he went above and beyond.

Now – let's say you got a room full of women. All you got to do is mention the words 'baby shower' - and they will somehow mysteriously start breaking up into subcommittees. Women will plan that sucker down to the last detail. I mean women will put more planning into a graduation party than General Norman Schwarzenegger put into invading Iraq.

An' it ain't just parties neither. Men don't want to plan nothing - including our own futures. Like last night down at the Duck Inn, my buddy Pete asks me, 'Hey, Earl, you got a retirement plan?' I go, 'Well – I got some money set aside… but to call it a 'plan' – would be a little like calling Rosie O'Donnell a super-model. Somebody would be grossly exaggerating. Or… sadly mistaken.

Wake up, America! Man Rule # 92 - Men are capable of planning the big things. Like D-Day. Everything else - we like to take on the fly. I'm Earl Pitts, American. Pitts Off.

'Women think men don't like to plan - because we're lazy. Nope - we just like surprises.'

MAN RULE # 61

Being called a 'cowboy' is never an insult.

You know what makes me sick? You know what makes me so mad I just wanna bull-ride - a grizzly bear?

Here's my question today - what the hell happened to America? Maybe I was dreaming... but I seem to remember when we were the world's super power. I remember when whatever America said - went. I remember when we could just look at another country funny - and make them flinch.

Today - our President goes to one of those G-8 or NATO meetings or whatever... and chances are he's the guy walking out of the meeting with a 'kick me' sign on his back. There's just this weird feeling like we may have lost the respect of the world.

Now - back when George Bush was president... everybody said we were 'cowboys'. America was acting like 'cowboys'. George Bush was a 'cowboy'.

When did being called a 'cowboy' become an insult? Don't you all wish we were cowboys again?

First of all - you knuckle-dragging, mouth-breathing nincompoops... this is America. Being a cowboy is good. Cowboys were John Wayne, Gary Cooper, the Outlaw Josey Wales... and Walker, Texas Ranger. Cowboys punched doggies, drove cattle up the trail to the

railhead, fought hand-to-hand combat with the Indians…
and conquered the west.

Cowboys were hard as rock, steady as steel - and honest
as the day is long. They took a bunch of worthless land
from the natives and carved it and shaped it into America.
They were tough enough to wrestle a bear. Quick enough
to snap a rattlesnake in half. And tender enough to
smooth-talk a school marm out of her petticoats. That
was a cowboy.

A cowboy's word was his bond… and his handshake was
his contract. He was slow to anger - but then quick on the
trigger. He slept under the stars… and stood guard over
America.

And he had a harmonica.

Wake up, America! Man Rule # 61 - Yeah - when those
foreign pant-loads and dope-smoking liberal idiots
convinced us being cowboys was a bad thing - they
sucked the *America* right out of America. Bring the
cowboy back! I'm Earl Pitts, American. Pitts Off.

**'Do whatever you can to remind people being a
'cowboy' is a good thing.
Like greet everyone with 'Howdy!' It's not much -
but it's a start.**

MAN RULE # 139

You can't fight terror - when you're still fighting stupid.

You know what makes me sick? You know what makes me so mad I just wanna pinch Joe Biden - to see if he's dreaming?   Because nobody that dumb can get that high up… in the real world.

Today I want to talk about America. On account of - the President wants us to fight this newest bunch of crazy-ass, whacked-out terror idiots. And we can't seem to get past fighting each other.

Yeah - I heard this from Bill O'Reilly. And I think we can all agree - Bill O'Reilly is kind of like the Alfred Einstein of politics. The boy's a genius. And Bill says America is more divided now than it has ever been.

Of course - we have been divided before. Like back in the Civil War. Or back in the 'Tastes Great - Less Filling' days. But the fact is - we're pretty divided.

The way I see it - there are two kinds of people in America today.   First - there's the right-thinking, hard-working, flag-waving, god-fearing, red-blooded, regular American. Or as I like to call them - my group. These are the people that suck it up - and get it done. These are the soldiers and the farmers… the truck drivers and factory workers and waitresses that put in a honest day's work and thank the good Lord every day that they live in the land of the free - and the home of the brave.

And then there's the other people. That would be the left-thinking, hardly-working, flag-burning, god-denying, pin-headed Americans. Or as I like to call them - Whiners, wussies and worry-warts.

These would be your George Clooneys… your Michael Moores, your Dixie Chicks and all those other commie sympathizing pinkos. These are the mouth-breathing liberals that figure whatever happens - we got it coming. And they worry what people in Europe will think.

Let me tell you something… worrying about what Europe thinks… is a little bit like the Fonz trying to get a thumbs-up from Potsie. That don't happen in the real world neither.

Wake up, America! Man Rule # 139 - My question is this - how are we gonna defeat radical Arab terrorism - when we're still fighting each other. It's tough to beat evil… when you're still fighting stupid. Let's all suck it up - come together - and do this thing. I'm Earl Pitts, American. Pitts Off.

'People ask me all the time, 'Earl, after all these years and all the things that have
passed - is it okay to like the Dixie Chicks again?'
No.

MAN RULE # 58

Sometimes we're offended - by people who are offended. Get a life.

You know what makes me sick? You know what makes me so mad I just wanna snap the beak off a wood-pecker? Then when he starts beating his head against a tree-trunk... he'll know how I feel living in America sometimes.

Yeah - I guess you seen where the government is tightening the screws on the Washington Redskins. If you been following this - some people think the name *Washington Redskins* is offensive to Indians. Well - everybody *except* the majority of Indians. Which is curious - but that's how it works in America these days. We're so big-hearted... we feel offended for other people.

So now the US trademark people have took the Redskins trademark away from the owner of the team. Now - I think y'all know me. I don't want to offend anybody - but this might be taking it too far. So I called a meeting of my organization - People Offended by Offended People... or POOP for short. We had the meeting on my Facebook page... and asked - 'If they can take away your name because it offends people... what other names are in danger?'

I started the ball rolling with the Cleveland Indians... Red Man tobacco... Indian Motorcycles... and of course, TV's lovable Wonder Years actor, Fred Savage. They would all have to change their names.

Several members of POOP... or as I like to call them - 'Poopies'... mentioned that the offensive part of the Washington Redskins name - might actually be 'Washington'. On account of it reminds hard-working, flag-waving regular Americans of - well, *Washington.* Then a guy named Marty said George Washington was also a wealthy white man who owned slaves, grew hemp and sold whiskey. Right there you're offending poor people, black people and Mothers Against Drunk Driving.

John said the Dallas Cowboys offended Indians... on account of Cowboys killed Indians. Well - that - and because Tony Romo sucks. Kimberly wondered if the St. Louis Cardinals weren't secretly religious... which would be a violation of church and sports. And Wayne says skiers all over the world feel threatened by the Colorado Avalanche.

Trademark department - we got a lot of work to do.

Wake up, America! Man Rule # 58 - I'm reminded what my great, great grandpa Abraham Lincoln Pitts once said. 'You can offend some of the people all of the time. And you can offend all of the people some of the time. But you can't offend anybody who has something better to do.' Think about it. I'm Earl Pitts, American. Pitts Off.

MAN RULE # 15

Respect a man who knows how to do stuff.
There's so few of us left.

You know what makes me sick? You know what makes me so mad I just wanna staple the helpful hardware guy to a stack of sheet rock - with a nail gun?

Today, I want to pay tribute to a dying species. The noble and majestic American Handyman.

I am an American Handyman - one of the last of my breed. Now let me take you back - and see if this don't sound familiar.

Back when we were kids - everybody's Daddy was a handyman. That is a do-it-yourself dad. One weekend, he'd be in the garage dropping the tranny on the family station wagon. The next weekend he'd be installing a new hot water heater. Basically - our daddies were the jack of all trades. They could fix it... repair it... install it... or rebuild it. And that knowledge was there for the taking.

But my generation? Apparently only half of us were paying attention. Lucky for me - I soaked up the knowledge like a shop rag sopping up an oil spill. And I thank my daddy for making me the handyman I am today. I can lay linoleum... seam drywall... wire up a breaker box. I'm a plumber... an auto mechanic. I can mix cement... hang a door... replace a window. I can trench, wire, paint, putty, spackle, shingle... you name it - I can do it. Even if I can't do it - I'll give it a shot. And chances are - I CAN do it.

So here is my problem with all of this. Let's say a true American original handyman - like myself... was to need something for a job I was doing. That means I got to go to the giant name-brand hardware store. People - them stores today - those aren't hardware stores. Those are giant decorating ant-hills for yuppies. You can stand right there in the parking lot and watch the yuppies streaming in and out of there carrying stuff. And none of it fixes nothing. It just 'remodels' stuff.

If you go in there carrying a chunk a metal you tore off the back end of your furnace - some clueless genius in a colorful vest will look at it... hold it up... stare at it for a few minutes... and go, 'Are you sure you don't want to see our winder coverings...?'

Wake up, America! Man Rule # 15 - We don't need a gum-smacking girl asking us if we need help. We need that 90-year old stooped-over guy that comes out of the back room holding up a piece of metal, and saying...'I think this will work.' That's the Handyman Yoda. I'm Earl Pitts, American. Pitts Off.

> **'If you want to see an American handyman swell up with pride - tell him you don't know how to fix something. And buy some beer.'**

If you see something that you
think looks stupid - it is.
Always go with your first impression.

Just because we ask, 'How you doin'?' doesn't
mean we actually want to know.

If the convenience store doesn't carry it -
you don't need it.

Always remember - for some reason, the police
seem to frown on 12-year old designated drivers.

MAN RULE # 4

No matter what the NFL would have you believe - never touch another man's butt.

You know what makes me sick? You know what makes me so mad I just wanna go ahead and have that snowball fight with Randy Johnson? Except – instead of snow… use croquet balls!!!

My old lady is so dumb sometimes. I mean, the woman makes Kim Kardashian look like a brain surgeon. She asks the stupidest questions. Like – I was watching a game the other night… and she goes, 'Earl – how come athletes like to spank each other's butt when they do something good?'

See what I mean? She don't understand the manly expression of joy. She doesn't understand the traditional art of the macho congratulations. She doesn't get the concept of teammates.

And then the more I thought about it – I don't understand it either.

Let me put it this way - I could make a list right now of 100 things I'd like to touch - and I'm fairly certain another man's butt would not be on the list. And it ain't like I never played sports… like I never got excited and congratulated a teammate. I just never grabbed another man's butt. And between you and me - I say that with a fair amount of pride.

Like at the bowling alley. When we pull off a beer frame - we'll high-five, low-five, give each other some skin... shake hands, knuckle bump, back-slap, chest thump. We'll hoot... we'll holler. We'll act like monkeys on crack. But we ain't touching each other's butts. I figure I want to congratulate a guy... I don't want to move in together and adopt a child!!

So it's not like I'm 'anti-congratulations'. I'm just a big believer in personal space. Which to me is everything inside the strike zone... knees to the nipples.

But there they are on the TV. You hit a three-pointer... score a touchdown... hit a homerun... and the rest of the team is lining up to cop a feel. Hey - how do you think Goose Gossage got his name.

Wake up, America! Man Rule # 4 - Before you congratulate your team mate... ask yourself - 'Is this how I would celebrate with a professional bull-riders... or Chuck Norris?' If the answer is no - then don't. I'm Earl Pitts, American. Pitts Off.

'If you congratulated Chuck Norris with a smack on the butt - you'd likely take a boot to the face. Treat every man like he was Chuck Norris.'

MAN RULE # 456

Don't be afraid of your emotions.
Just ignore them.

You know what makes me sick? You know what makes me so mad I just wanna squirm around naked... on sandpaper?

I hate when some of you touchy-feely, kumbaya-jerks out there don't think I – Earl Pitts – have no emotional depth. I get these emails all the time – 'Earl, you are a Neanderthal. Earl Pitts is a senseless clod..' And those are just the comments I get from my own family. Total strangers can be much harsher.

So to prove to y'all that I have a sensitive and emotional core... I am gonna tell you the story about me putting my dog down. Yeah – I had an old dog one time. He was lame in one leg after getting hit by a car... blind in one eye because the neighbor kid shot it out with a B-B gun... and he only had one ear due to an unfortunate accident with a weed-whacker. My dog's name was Lucky. And after several years of limping around, walking into doors and not hearing us call him to dinner – Lucky's robust health began to fade.

I took him to the vet - but they said there was nothing they could do. So I took him home and kind of babied him for a couple months. It got to where he couldn't hardly even stand up. So I knew what I had to do. I put old Lucky in the truck for one last ride. I was gonna have the doctor put him down.

In the truck - Lucky kind of lifted up his head from the front seat there and gave me a look – that said he understood. And he kind of rubbed his nose on my leg. It was like he was either forgiving me... or thanking me for what I was doing. He was in a lot of pain.

And I started bawling like a baby. Lucky just looked at me... with his good eye, of course. Hell – I couldn't even see the road no more – my eyeballs was so full of tears. So I pulled over to the side of the highway... and I carried Lucky to a grassy spot there... and I hugged him... and we both said goodbye.

Then I fished a tennis ball out of my jacket pocket and threw it across the Interstate. Lucky never knew what hit him. I think it was a late-model Chrysler, if I can remember correctly.

Wake up, America! Man Rule # 456 - Sure it was emotional. But it was 50-bucks cheaper, too... which was a lot of money back then. But it still hurt. Just not financially. I'm Earl Pitts, American. Pitts Off.

MAN RULE # 167

Real men don't stand in line.

You know what makes me sick? You know what makes me so mad I just wanna go down to the Boy's and Girl's Club - and punch orphans?

Yeah – no real man wants to stand in no stupid line. End of story. See, my old lady and the neighbor-lady Naomi are already talking about what discount store they want to stand in line for on Thanksgiving night. And my little boy, Earl Jr. and a couple a' his pimple-faced idiot buddies say they're gonna stand in line at the video game store for some dimwit new video game they got coming out.

That's when I decided to come up with a list of things I WILL NOT stand in line for. And it's a pretty big list. I will not stand in line for a stupid new phone... a stupid new movie... a stupid sale... some stupid government hand-out... to see some stupid banshee screaming idiot singer and her stupid loser band. Why? Because that's stupid.

I will not stand in line to be the first to buy anything... see anything... or go anywhere. And I sure as hell ain't gonna stand in line for a chance to see some high-horse political pant-load... and shake his hand. I will not stand in line to take a leak – if the line is outside and there is a tree, an alley or a parked car nearby.

People ask me all the time – 'Earl, how come you don't fly?' Number one – because there's no place I want to go. Number two – I don't want to stand in line. I don't want to stand in line at the bank... at the grocery store... and especially not at the DMV. I know guys still in line at the DMV – that got in the line – back in May. I'd rather pay the fine and court fees. And possibly a small amount of jail time.

In fact – I hate lines so much... if the good Lord pulled my number right now... and there was a line at the Pearly Gates - I might think twice. Of course the way this world's going - there's a good chance the line down below – is a lot longer. So, then again- I might think twice – about thinking twice.

Obviously you've got to be thinking... 'Earl, is there anything you WOULD stand in line for?' The only thing I can think of involves Shania Twain and a cowboy water trough full of Cool Whip. So I might as well just answer no. Because there'd be a real long line to see that, too.

Wake up, America! Man Rule # 167 - When a woman tells her husband, 'Hurry up - get in line!' What he hears is 'Hurry up - surrender your soul.' Women - we are like wild stallions - we cannot be corralled by waist high posts and black cloth. I'm Earl Pitts, America. Pitts Off.

MAN RULE # 74

Keep your pants on. I mean - *literally* - keep your pants on!!

You know what makes me sick? You know what makes me so mad I just wanna chew the legs off a wrought iron table?

Now – I'm going to say something controversial here - so don't go getting your panties in a wad and acting like I kicked your cat. It's just an observation on my part.

There's too many naked people in the world. Like some evil genius computer hacker – hacked Hollywood. And he didn't find a couple of naked photos of some nubile and chesty young Hollywood starlet to post on that World Wide Internet. No sir. He found *thousands* of photos of *hundreds* of naked starlets!! And nobody was surprised.

Then you got your naked TV shows... *Naked & Afraid. Naked Dating...* And of course, *360 with Anderson Cooper.* I don't know what in the blazes he's thinking.

Those twisted perverts at PETA – they don't want you to wear fur... so what do they do? Get a couple of long-legged super-models to walk around naked. That makes total sense, right? Here's a big thing now – an annual naked bicycle ride - all over the world. I thought that might be interesting. But then again - think about what could get caught in the chain!! Yikes. They even got a day in New York City where everybody rides the subway without pants on. I know they call it the Big Apple. But that doesn't mean we want to see your banana.

It used to be - if you wanted to see naked people... you needed a dirty book store... pay cable... or a strip club. Hell – now skin – is in! Buck naked is main-stream.

And for the life of me... I have never once looked at myself in the bathroom mirror after taking a shower and thought... 'Now THIS is something I want to share with the rest of the world.' Because like 99.9% of the world... I do not have a naked-friendly body. And I got news for you – unless you're a nubile, chesty Hollywood starlet – or a leggy super-model... you don't neither.

Wake up, America! Man Rule # 74 - All I'm saying is... it's best to leave nudity to the professionals. Because amateurs without pants – is not a pretty sight. I'm Earl Pitts, American. Pitts Off.

**'There are a lot of naked people out there that could use a sense of decency and self-respect.
Or - at the very least - a mirror.'**

MAN RULE # 182

If you can't get even - at least get mad

You know what makes me sick? You know what makes me so mad I just wanna take a deep breath... count to ten... and then put my boot so far up somebody's hind-end - the next time they sneeze - shoe-laces will come out of their nose???

Yeah - did you see where before the election - some of those four-eyed geniuses did one of those doofus, cockamamie telephone poll deals... and seven out of ten Americans said - they were angry for this election? Yeah - seven out of ten Americans are mad at the way the country is going... mad at politicians... and mad at the President.

Ladies and gentlemen - I would just like to say - welcome to my world. When it comes to being mad at the way things are - I'm what your marketing boys call - an early adopter. I'm a little like Barbara Mandrel. Hell - I was angry back when angry wasn't cool.

Call it whatever you want - going off the deep end. Going postal. Hitting the wall. Going nuts. I'm like a bad wheel on Dale Jr's car. I'm about to fly off and hurt someone.

And can we all agree - this has not been a good year to get over it. It kind of hit me this morning when I was stopping for coffee. And Runt Wilson was in there pouring hisself a cup of coffee, too. And he goes, 'How's it going, Earl?'

Well - I could not pass up the opportunity. I unloaded on the boy. I go, 'My boss is on my butt. My wife is on my back. And my kids are on my nerves. My back aches. My head hurts. And I got a hemorrhoid the size of a VW Beetle. I got iron-poor blood, a cash-poor bank account. My house is a dump, my truck is a junker... and my neighbors are all idiots. I said, 'My town is a joke... my prospects are limited... and this morning my old lady thought she was coming down with Ebola. My own government is out to get me... if those crazy-butt, knuckle-dragging terrorists don't get me first. I go... 'It's like life is one big steaming pile of crap... and I'm ankle deep in it. How 'bout you, Runt?'

He puts the lid on his coffee and he looks at me and goes... 'Bout the same...'

Wake up, America! Man Rule # 182 - Don't forget to vent. Yeah - seven out of ten Americans are now mad. Like I said - welcome to my world. I'm Earl Pitts, American. And Pitts Off.

'Don't forget - letting off a little steam is better than letting your brain explode.'

MAN RULE # 2

Remember - the way things were - are always better than the way things are.

You know what makes me sick? You know what makes me so mad - I just wanna trim my nose-hairs... with a weed-whacker?

Today we're not here to belly-ache or complain. Today - I want to sing the praises of a true American. A man's man, and true hero in every town, hamlet, village and city in this country.

Today - let's take a minute and thank - the barber.

And I'm not talking about those prissy-pants hair salon boys - I'm talking about an honest to goodness, wrap some toilet paper around your neck and start mowing - barber. I'm talking about the kind of guy what will stand eight hours on his feet six days a week - shaving the old man wire off the edges of your ears... all the while he's telling you the filthiest jokes this side of a biker bar.

I'm talking about the kind of guy that give some air-head idiot kid a buzz-cut in a minute flat... and then take a whole half-hour making some old boy's comb-over look just perfect.

The barber is the only guy in town that has the whole skinny on who's hiring and who's laying off. He can talk muscle cars, high school sports, church gossip and town politics. If you hear a bunch of sirens in the middle of the night and don't know what happened - wake up the next morning - and go get a haircut.

And for a real man - these is no more comfortable place on this earth than a real barbershop. Big comfortable chairs up against the wall... a TV up near the ceiling that only gets four channels. A dog-eared Field & Stream magazine you remember already reading when you were in there - ten years ago! You got farmers and truckers in there - shooting the breeze. Others kind of zoned out - just setting there, watching the hair hit the floor. Nobody passes judgment on nobody. You all want the same thing - a haircut. It's like a man cave - for actual men.

And the best part is when you get in the chair. Because the barber doesn't even ask what you want. Because he already knows what you need. Just lower the ears.

Wake up, America! Man Rule # 2 - Every time you step into a barber shop - you feel like you're back in 'real America.' Sadly - the American barber is like the buffalo - a vanishing breed. The day the last American barber leaves this world - is the day I start a pony-tail. I'm Earl Pitts, American. Pitts off.

MAN RULE # 119

Never pass up an opportunity - even the gross ones

You know what makes me sick? You know what makes me so mad I just wanna go to the North Pole and sucker-punch elves?

Y'all seen where Jose Canseco is selling his middle finger? It's true. For those of you that don't know - Jose Canseco was a steroid-sucking super-star of the baseball field. Maybe a touch on the dense side - but he did hit 462 homeruns. But then he became stoolie after he retired and admitted he was doping - and named names of other dopers, too.

So now - the boy was cleaning his gun about a month ago and shot off his finger. Figuring he already shot off his mouth - what's one more body part, right? The doctors reattached it... but it fell off again. This is the point where you have to remember I mentioned Jose Canseco might be a little dense - because he said he was going to sell his middle finger - on the Internet.

And I intend to buy it.

Now - people are asking me - 'Earl - what can you do - with Jose Canseco's middle finger?' To me - it's more a question of - what *can't* you do?

Number one - I can pick my nose while watching TV. And when my old lady goes, 'Get your finger out of your nose - that's disgusting.' I'll just say, 'It's not my finger. It's Jose Canseco's finger. '

Number two - I can flip off people in traffic. And when some burly-butt redneck tracks me down and gets up in my face... wanting to know how come I made an obscene gesture. I'll just say - 'You got the wrong guy, mister. It wasn't me. It was Jose Canseco.'

Number three - I can go on a cross-country crime-spree... and leave Jose Canseco fingerprints. I could do the crime... and Jose Canseco can do the time.

Number four - I could take Jose Canseco's finger to wherever they got Ted Williams' head... and stick it in the freezer with Ted's head. Hopefully someday science will be advanced enough... they could bring back a whole outfield.

Wake up, America! Man Rule #119 - If a famous person is willing to give you the finger - take it. I looked it up - that's 983 homeruns - in one freezer!! Not bad for body-parts. And people think I'm crazy. Yeah - crazy smart!! I'm Earl Pitts, American. Pitts Off.

If you blow something big time -
blame it on getting older.

If you have to wear a suit and tie for your job -
get another job.

Bacon can't fix everything that's
wrong in the world.
But that doesn't mean you shouldn't try it.

Don't forget to thank the man upstairs -
for not River Dancing in his living room while
you were trying to get some sleep.

Earl Pitts, American - has been entertaining radio listeners for thirty years. He meets with Radio Hall of Famer, Gary Burbank and writer, Tim Mizak regularly down at the Duck Inn. They help him find his voice and put his thoughts into words.

On The Internet:

Contact me by e-mail:
earl@earlpittsamerican.com

Website: earlpittsamerican.com
Facebook: facebook.com/earlpittsamerican
Twitter: twitter.com/earlpittsoff
Instagram: @earlpittsamerican
Youtube: youtube.com/earlpittsamerican

By Mail:

Wake Up Radio, Inc
8022 South Rainbow Blvd
Suite 219
Las Vegas, NV 89139

iTunes

If you are missing Earl Pitts and your
radio station doesn't carry me go to
iTunes and download all of my latest
commentaries.

Amazon

Get my other book titled Wake Up
America!!! at amazon.com